Chapter 1: Understanding Bipolar Disorder

What is Bipolar Disorder?

Bipolar disorder is a mental health condition characterized by significant mood swings, including emotional highs known as mania or hypomania and lows referred to as depression. These shifts can impact a person's energy levels, activity, judgment, and the ability to think clearly. While the exact cause of bipolar disorder is not fully understood, it is believed to involve a combination of genetic, biochemical, and environmental factors. Recognizing the symptoms and understanding the nature of the disorder is an essential first step in building a stable and fulfilling life.

During manic or hypomanic episodes, individuals may feel euphoric, full of energy, or unusually irritable. They might engage in impulsive behaviors, make rapid decisions, and experience racing thoughts. Conversely, depressive episodes can bring about feelings of hopelessness, fatigue, and a loss of interest in activities once enjoyed. These contrasting states can be disorienting and overwhelming. However, it is important to remember that experiencing these fluctuations does not define you; they are part of a medical condition that can be managed with the right strategies and support.

Living with bipolar disorder can often feel isolating, but you are not alone in this journey. Many people share similar experiences, and understanding that this condition affects millions can be comforting. The key to navigating bipolar disorder lies in developing coping strategies that work for you. This may include therapy, medication, lifestyle changes, and building a strong support network. Each individual's experience is unique, and finding the right combination of tools can empower you to take control of your life.

Establishing a routine can be particularly beneficial in managing bipolar disorder. Consistency provides a sense of stability and can help mitigate the intensity of mood swings. Incorporating regular sleep patterns, balanced nutrition, and physical activity into your daily life can create a solid foundation for emotional well-being. Additionally, practicing mindfulness techniques such as meditation or deep-breathing exercises can help ground you during challenging moments. These small, manageable changes can lead to significant improvements in your overall mental health.

As you navigate the complexities of bipolar disorder, remember that progress takes time and patience. Celebrate your achievements, no matter how small, and be gentle with yourself during setbacks. Building stability in your life is a journey, and each step forward is a testament to your resilience. With the right mindset and a toolkit of coping strategies, you can create a fulfilling life that embraces both your challenges and your strengths. You have the power to cultivate a steady ground beneath your feet.

The Impact of Bipolar Disorder on Daily Life

Living with bipolar disorder can create unique challenges that affect daily life in profound ways. Fluctuating moods can disrupt routines, impact relationships, and influence one's ability to maintain employment or pursue personal interests. Recognizing these challenges is the first step toward developing coping strategies that can help you navigate the ups and downs of this condition. It's important to remember that while bipolar disorder may shape your experiences, it does not define your capabilities or your worth.

One of the most significant impacts of bipolar disorder is the effect it has on relationships. Mood swings can lead to misunderstandings and strain between family members, friends, and romantic partners. During manic episodes, increased energy and impulsivity may result in erratic behavior, while depressive phases can lead to withdrawal and isolation. However, open communication with loved ones about your feelings and experiences can help bridge the gap. Seeking support from those who understand your journey fosters connection and can alleviate feelings of loneliness that often accompany the disorder.

Employment can also be influenced by bipolar disorder. The challenge of maintaining consistent performance can be daunting, especially when mood fluctuations disrupt focus and motivation. Creating a structured routine can be invaluable in managing daily tasks and responsibilities. Establishing a supportive work environment, whether through flexible hours or the option to work remotely, can also enhance productivity. Remember, many individuals with bipolar disorder excel in their careers by embracing their unique perspective and creativity. Finding a job that aligns with your strengths and passions can lead to fulfilling work experiences.

Incorporating self-care practices into your daily life can significantly improve your overall well-being. Regular exercise, a balanced diet, and sufficient sleep play crucial roles in mood stabilization. Mindfulness techniques, such as meditation or journaling, can also provide valuable tools for managing stress and enhancing emotional regulation. These practices don't just help mitigate the impact of bipolar disorder; they also empower you to take an active role in your mental health. Small, consistent efforts can lead to meaningful changes over time, fostering a sense of control and resilience.

Lastly, it is essential to cultivate a mindset of hope and acceptance. Living with bipolar disorder can be challenging, but it also offers opportunities for personal growth and self-discovery. Embracing your journey, with all of its ups and downs, allows for a more profound understanding of yourself. Connecting with support groups or engaging with others who share similar experiences can provide encouragement and insight. Remember, you are not alone in this journey, and each step you take toward understanding and managing your condition is a testament to your strength and determination.

Common Misconceptions

Many people hold misconceptions about bipolar disorder that can hinder understanding and support for those living with it. One common belief is that bipolar disorder is simply a matter of mood swings. While it is true that mood changes are a hallmark of the condition, the reality is much more complex. Individuals with bipolar disorder experience episodes of extreme highs (mania or hypomania) and lows (depression) that significantly disrupt their daily lives. Recognizing that these shifts are part of a broader spectrum of symptoms can help foster empathy and patience, both from oneself and from others.

Another prevalent misconception is that bipolar disorder is a rare condition. In truth, it affects millions of people worldwide, cutting across all demographics and backgrounds. This widespread prevalence means that you are not alone in your experiences. Connecting with others who share similar struggles can be immensely beneficial, providing a sense of community and understanding. By acknowledging that many people navigate similar challenges, individuals can find solace and strength in shared experiences, which can enhance their coping strategies.

Some might believe that bipolar disorder is solely a result of personal weakness or poor choices. This harmful notion can lead to feelings of shame and isolation for those affected. It's essential to remember that bipolar disorder is a medical condition, influenced by a combination of genetic, biological, and environmental factors. Understanding this can empower individuals to seek help and treatment without the burden of guilt. It opens the door to self-compassion, allowing individuals to view their struggles through a lens of care rather than judgment.

Additionally, many assume that once treatment is started, the struggles with bipolar disorder will cease entirely. While effective treatments, such as medication and therapy, can significantly improve symptoms, managing bipolar disorder often requires ongoing effort and adaptation. Fluctuations can still occur, and setbacks may happen. Embracing this reality can help individuals develop resilience and adaptability in their coping strategies. It's a journey, and recognizing that progress can be nonlinear can alleviate pressure and foster a more compassionate relationship with oneself.

Finally, there is a misconception that individuals with bipolar disorder cannot lead fulfilling, productive lives. This belief is far from the truth. With the right tools, support, and coping strategies, many people with bipolar disorder thrive in their personal and professional lives. They cultivate meaningful relationships, pursue passions, and achieve their goals. By focusing on strengths and potential rather than limitations, individuals can set their sights on a brighter future, encouraging themselves to take small, steady steps toward stability and fulfillment.

Chapter 2: Recognizing Patterns

Identifying Triggers

Identifying triggers is a crucial step in managing bipolar disorder effectively. Triggers can be anything from changes in routine, stress at work, interpersonal conflicts, or even changes in seasons. Understanding what specifically sets off mood swings allows you to take proactive measures to reduce their impact on your life. When you begin to recognize these patterns, it empowers you to develop coping strategies tailored to your unique experiences.

Start by keeping a mood journal. This tool can help you track your emotions, daily activities, and potential triggers over time. Make a habit of noting down any significant events or stressors you encounter and how they correlate with your mood changes. By identifying recurring themes or patterns, you can gain insight into what influences your mental state. This awareness is the first step toward taking control of your emotional health, allowing you to navigate through both the highs and lows with greater ease.

Consider engaging in reflective practices. Take time each day to sit quietly and reflect on your feelings and the circumstances surrounding them. Ask yourself questions about what might have led to a shift in your mood. Were you feeling overwhelmed? Did a particular situation or conversation affect you? Through this process, you may uncover specific triggers that you hadn't previously recognized. This self-reflection is not only enlightening but can be a powerful tool in your healing journey, providing clarity that leads to empowerment.

In addition to personal reflection, don't hesitate to seek support from friends, family, or mental health professionals. Sharing your experiences can provide new perspectives and help you identify triggers that may be less obvious to you. Others may notice changes in your behavior or mood that you might not recognize yourself. This collaborative approach not only strengthens your support network but also reinforces your resilience in managing your condition.

As you become more adept at identifying triggers, remember to practice self-compassion throughout the process. It's normal to have setbacks, and recognizing triggers is just one aspect of a larger journey toward stability. Celebrate the small victories, and remind yourself that every step taken toward understanding your triggers is a step toward a more balanced life. With patience and persistence, you can build a stable foundation that allows you to thrive, even amidst the challenges of bipolar disorder.

Understanding Mood Cycles

Understanding mood cycles is a crucial aspect of managing bipolar disorder. Recognizing the patterns of your mood swings can empower you to take control of your life and make informed choices about your well-being. Mood cycles often oscillate between depressive lows and manic highs, and being aware of these fluctuations allows you to prepare for the challenges they may bring. Instead of feeling overwhelmed by your emotions, you can learn to observe them as natural occurrences that you can navigate with awareness and resilience.

Each individual experiences mood cycles differently, and understanding your unique patterns is essential. Keeping a mood diary can be a valuable tool in this process. By recording your daily emotions, triggers, and behaviors, you can start to identify the signs that precede a shift in your mood. Over time, you may notice trends that can help you anticipate a change, allowing you to take proactive steps to manage your feelings. This awareness can foster a sense of control and reduce the fear that often accompanies unpredictable mood changes.

In addition to recognizing your own patterns, learning about the general phases of mood cycles can also provide insight. Typically, individuals with bipolar disorder may experience periods of mania characterized by increased energy, heightened creativity, and impulsivity, followed by depressive episodes marked by fatigue, hopelessness, and withdrawal. Understanding these phases can help you develop strategies tailored to each stage. For instance, during manic phases, you might focus on channeling that energy into productive activities, while during depressive episodes, you could prioritize self-care and seek support from loved ones.

Support systems play a vital role in navigating mood cycles. Connecting with others who understand your experiences can provide a sense of belonging and lessen feelings of isolation. Whether through support groups, therapy, or simply confiding in friends and family, sharing your journey can help you process your emotions and gain new perspectives. These connections can also serve as a safety net during challenging times, reminding you that you are not alone in your struggles and that there are people who care about your well-being.

Ultimately, understanding mood cycles is not just about recognizing the ups and downs of bipolar disorder; it is about fostering resilience and hope. It is possible to build stability in your life by implementing coping strategies that resonate with you. Embracing mindfulness, practicing self-compassion, and developing a routine can all contribute to a more balanced life. By actively engaging with your mood cycles and seeking support, you can create a foundation of strength and adaptability that allows you to thrive, even amidst the challenges of bipolar disorder.

Keeping a Mood Diary

Keeping a mood diary can be an incredibly empowering tool for individuals navigating the complexities of bipolar disorder. This practice allows you to document your emotions, triggers, and reactions over time, creating a clearer picture of your mental landscape. By regularly noting how you feel, you can identify patterns and gain insights that may otherwise remain hidden. This awareness is the first step toward developing strategies for managing your moods and making informed decisions about your care.

To begin, choose a format that works best for you. Some people prefer a physical notebook, while others may find digital apps more convenient. The key is to select a method that feels comfortable and accessible. Each entry should include the date, your mood rating on a scale from one to ten, and a brief description of what you experienced that day. Consider noting any significant events, interactions, or changes in your routine, as these can all impact your emotional state. Over time, you may notice recurring themes or triggers that can inform your coping strategies.

Consistency is crucial when maintaining a mood diary. Aim to make entries at the same time each day, whether it's in the morning to set intentions or in the evening to reflect on the day's events. This practice not only helps you stay accountable but also reinforces your commitment to understanding your mental health. As you establish this routine, remember to be gentle with yourself. There may be days when you struggle to find the words, and that's perfectly okay. The important thing is to keep coming back to the diary, allowing it to evolve as your journey unfolds.

Reviewing your entries regularly can be a transformative experience. Set aside time each week or month to look back on your mood patterns and identify any correlations. You might discover that certain activities, environments, or even people influence your moods positively or negatively. This reflection can empower you to make proactive choices, such as seeking more of what uplifts you and minimizing exposure to stressors. Sharing your insights with a therapist can further enhance your understanding and provide additional strategies tailored to your unique experiences.

Ultimately, keeping a mood diary is not just an exercise in tracking feelings; it's a powerful tool for self-discovery and growth. By fostering a deeper understanding of your emotional landscape, you can cultivate resilience and make informed choices that support your journey toward stability. Embrace this practice with an open heart, knowing that each entry brings you one step closer to living a balanced life amidst the challenges of bipolar disorder. Your commitment to this process is a testament to your strength and determination, and it can lead to profound personal insights that help guide you along your path.

Chapter 3: Building a Support System

The Importance of Support

Support plays a crucial role in navigating the complexities of bipolar disorder. For individuals grappling with the emotional highs and lows, having a reliable support system can make all the difference. Friends, family, and mental health professionals provide not only companionship but also understanding and validation. The journey can be isolating, but knowing that others care and are willing to walk alongside you fosters a sense of belonging. It reassures you that you are not alone in your struggles and encourages you to seek help when times get tough.

The importance of support extends beyond just emotional comfort. A strong support network can offer practical assistance during challenging times. This can include help with daily tasks, reminders for medication, or simply being there to listen when you need to express your feelings. These acts, though seemingly small, can alleviate some of the burdens that come with managing bipolar disorder. They create a safety net, allowing you to focus on your mental health without the added pressure of feeling overwhelmed by everyday responsibilities.

Moreover, support can also come in the form of peer groups or support groups specifically tailored for those with bipolar disorder. These gatherings provide a safe space to share experiences, exchange coping strategies, and gain insights from others who understand the unique challenges you face. Hearing stories of resilience from others can inspire hope and motivate you to adopt new coping techniques. You may discover that others have faced similar hurdles and have found ways to overcome them, which can lead to personal growth and a stronger sense of community.

It's essential to communicate your needs to those around you. Many people may want to help but may not know how to do so effectively. Being open about your experiences and what you find helpful can empower others to provide the support you need. This transparency not only strengthens your relationships but also fosters a deeper understanding among your loved ones about the intricacies of bipolar disorder. They can become advocates for you and assist in creating an environment that is conducive to your well-being.

Ultimately, support is about building connections that nurture and sustain you throughout your journey. Embracing the idea that you deserve help and encouragement is a powerful step toward stability. As you cultivate these relationships, remember that reaching out is a sign of strength, not weakness. With a solid support system in place, you can face the challenges of bipolar disorder with renewed confidence, knowing that you have allies by your side who are committed to your well-being.

Finding the Right People

Finding the right people to surround yourself with is a crucial step in navigating the complexities of bipolar disorder. The journey can often feel isolating, but the support system you build can provide stability and encouragement. Seek out individuals who understand your experiences, whether they are friends, family members, or fellow peers in the mental health community. These connections can help you feel less alone and remind you that you are not defined solely by your diagnosis.

Consider the qualities that make someone a good support person in your life. Look for those who are empathetic, patient, and willing to listen without judgment. You want people who encourage open communication, allowing you to express your feelings, whether you are feeling euphoric or experiencing a low. It can be beneficial to have friends or family who have some knowledge of bipolar disorder, as they may be more equipped to understand the nuances of your experience and respond appropriately during difficult times.

Engaging with support groups, either in person or online, can also be an excellent way to find the right people. These groups often consist of individuals who share similar struggles and triumphs. Hearing others' stories can offer insights and strategies that resonate with your own experiences. You'll likely find a sense of camaraderie and understanding in these spaces, which can be immensely comforting. Remember, building friendships in these environments might take time, but the bonds formed can be incredibly supportive.

It's equally important to establish boundaries with those who may not be equipped to handle the emotional complexities of bipolar disorder. While it can be painful to distance yourself from certain relationships, protecting your mental health should be a priority. Surrounding yourself with people who uplift you and contribute positively to your life can foster a sense of safety and stability. You deserve relationships that are nurturing and respectful, where you feel empowered to be your authentic self.

As you embark on the journey of finding the right people, remember that this process is not just about seeking support but also about being a supportive person in return. Building mutual relationships where both parties feel valued can create a strong foundation. Celebrate the connections you form and nurture them with honesty, compassion, and understanding. With the right people by your side, navigating life with bipolar disorder can become more manageable, allowing you to focus on your growth and well-being.

Communicating Your Needs

Communicating your needs effectively is a vital skill on the journey of managing bipolar disorder. Many individuals find it challenging to express their feelings and requirements, often fearing misunderstanding or rejection. However, being open about your needs can foster stronger relationships and create a support system that understands your unique experiences. Remember, your feelings and needs are valid, and articulating them is an essential step toward self-advocacy and wellness.

Begin by identifying what you need in different situations. This process can involve reflecting on your emotions, triggers, and the support you seek from others. Whether you need someone to listen, help with daily tasks, or simply some space to recharge, understanding your own needs is the first step to communicating them. Journaling can be an effective tool for this; jot down your thoughts and feelings regularly, helping you clarify what you might want to express to those around you.

Once you have a clearer understanding of your needs, practice articulating them in a calm and direct manner. Choose a time when you feel stable and relaxed to have these conversations. Use "I" statements to express your feelings without placing blame or making others defensive. For instance, saying "I feel overwhelmed and need some quiet time" can open the door to understanding, while also allowing others to respond with empathy and support. Remember that it's okay to ask for what you need; you deserve to have your requirements acknowledged.

Encouraging open lines of communication with friends, family, and healthcare providers can also enhance your support network. Let them know that you are navigating bipolar disorder and that there may be times when you need extra understanding or adjustments in your interactions. By educating your loved ones about your condition, you can foster a more empathetic environment, making it easier for them to respond to your needs appropriately.

Lastly, don't be afraid to reassess and adjust your needs as your circumstances change. Bipolar disorder can present fluctuating challenges, and what you require may shift over time. Regularly check in with yourself and those around you to ensure that your needs are still being met. This ongoing dialogue will not only strengthen your relationships but also empower you to take charge of your mental health journey. Remember that you are not alone in this process; communicating your needs is a sign of strength and a crucial part of building a stable and fulfilling life.

Chapter 4: Coping Strategies

Mindfulness and Meditation

Mindfulness and meditation serve as powerful tools for individuals navigating the complexities of bipolar disorder. These practices offer a way to cultivate awareness of thoughts, emotions, and bodily sensations, allowing for a deeper understanding of oneself. By focusing on the present moment, mindfulness helps reduce the overwhelming feelings that often accompany mood swings. This simple yet profound shift in awareness can create a sense of stability, empowering you to respond to challenges rather than react impulsively.

Incorporating mindfulness into your daily routine doesn't require extensive training or experience. Start with just a few minutes each day, finding a quiet space where you can sit comfortably. Close your eyes and focus on your breath, noticing the rise and fall of your chest. When your mind wanders, gently bring your attention back to your breath. This practice may seem challenging at first, but with patience and consistency, it can become a grounding ritual that enhances your overall emotional regulation.

Setting aside time for prayer daily can also be very helpful, especially in the morning before your day gets started. This can help set the mood for your entire day. Prayer offers a comforting way to connect with God and seek His guidance. For some people prayer provides a deep sense of peace and understanding. In quiet moments of prayer, individuals may feel a profound sense of connection to something larger than themselves, God. Through prayer, people can express their hopes, fears, and desires to a divine God who cares for them. The act of praying can instill a sense of hope and optimism, even in the face of challenges. Countless individuals have shared stories of finding comfort and relief through prayer during difficult times. For many, prayer has been a source of strength and resilience, helping them too overcome obstacles and find meaning in their lives. When you are feeling lost or out of control, you can pause and pray for peace and comfort and believe that God is there and will help you through your difficult time. Many people feel a great comfort knowing that they are never completely alone and that God is there to reach out to for help.

Meditation, a more structured form of mindfulness, can further deepen your ability to maintain stability. Guided meditations, available through various apps and online resources, can provide direction and support as you explore this practice. Consider setting aside time each day to engage in meditation, allowing yourself to connect with your inner self. Over time, you may find that meditation helps you cultivate a sense of calm, helping to balance the emotional highs and lows often experienced in bipolar disorder.

As you progress on your mindfulness and meditation journey, celebrate the small victories. Each moment of awareness or clarity is a step forward in building resilience. Keep in mind that it's normal to face challenges along the way; the key is to approach these obstacles with kindness and patience towards yourself. Remember that mindfulness is not about achieving perfection but rather about embracing the process of self-discovery and growth.

Ultimately, mindfulness and meditation can serve as essential components of your coping strategies. They can enhance your ability to manage stress, improve your mood, and promote a sense of inner peace. By committing to these practices, you are investing in your well-being and nurturing a more stable foundation for your life with bipolar disorder. Embrace the journey, and trust that each moment spent in mindfulness brings you closer to the steady ground you seek.

Exercise and Physical Health

Exercise is a powerful tool that can significantly enhance physical health, especially for those navigating the challenges of bipolar disorder. Engaging in regular physical activity can lead to improved mood regulation and increased energy levels. When you incorporate exercise into your routine, you may find that it not only helps to alleviate some symptoms of bipolar disorder but also enhances your overall well-being. It's important to remember that even small amounts of movement can have a positive impact, so finding an activity you enjoy can make all the difference.

One of the most profound effects of exercise is its ability to release endorphins, often referred to as "feel-good" hormones. These endorphins can create a natural sense of euphoria and reduce feelings of anxiety and depression. For someone managing bipolar disorder, this boost can be especially beneficial during challenging times. Whether it's a brisk walk, a dance class, or a yoga session, discovering what makes you feel good can empower you to seek out those moments of joy more frequently.

Establishing a consistent exercise routine can also promote better sleep patterns, which is crucial for maintaining emotional stability. Many individuals with bipolar disorder experience sleep disturbances, and regular physical activity can help regulate your sleep cycle. Aim for a balance that works for you—whether it's moderate exercise during the day or gentle stretching before bed. Creating a routine around physical activity can establish a sense of normalcy, offering structure that can be particularly comforting during manic or depressive episodes.

In addition to the physical benefits, exercise can foster a sense of community and connection. Joining a local fitness class, participating in group sports, or even engaging in outdoor activities with friends can provide valuable social support. This sense of belonging can alleviate feelings of isolation that often accompany bipolar disorder, reminding you that you are not alone in your journey. Building relationships through shared activities can enhance your mood and provide an additional layer of stability.

Finally, it's essential to approach exercise with a mindset of self-compassion. Recognizing that there will be days when motivation wanes and energy levels fluctuate is key. On those days, gentle movement or simply taking a walk outside can be enough. Celebrate your efforts, no matter how small, and understand that progress is not always linear. By integrating exercise into your life in a way that feels sustainable and enjoyable, you can cultivate resilience and support your journey toward a more stable, fulfilling life.

Sleep Hygiene

Sleep hygiene is a crucial aspect of managing bipolar disorder, as it can significantly influence mood stability. Establishing a consistent sleep routine is one of the most effective strategies for improving overall well-being. Aim to go to bed and wake up at the same time every day, even on weekends. This consistency helps regulate your body's internal clock, making it easier to fall asleep and wake up refreshed. Preparing for sleep should be a calming ritual; consider activities like reading, gentle stretching, or meditation to signal to your body that it's time to wind down.

Create a sleep-friendly environment that promotes relaxation. Your bedroom should be a sanctuary, free from distractions such as screens and loud noises. Darkness is essential for quality sleep, so consider blackout curtains or an eye mask. The temperature of your room plays a significant role too; a cool and comfortable environment can help facilitate better sleep. Finally, investing in a comfortable mattress and pillows can make a considerable difference in your ability to rest well each night.

Be mindful of your intake of food and beverages, particularly in the hours leading up to bedtime. Caffeine and nicotine can disrupt your ability to fall asleep, so it's advisable to limit these substances in the afternoon and evening. Alcohol may seem like a quick fix for relaxation, but it can lead to fragmented sleep. Instead, consider herbal teas or warm milk as soothing alternatives that can promote a sense of calm before bed. Eating a light snack can also be beneficial, but try to avoid heavy meals that can lead to discomfort and keep you awake.

Incorporating physical activity into your daily routine can greatly enhance your sleep quality. Regular exercise helps reduce anxiety and stress, both of which can interfere with your ability to sleep. Aim for at least 30 minutes of moderate exercise most days, but be mindful of timing; vigorous workouts close to bedtime may have the opposite effect. Instead, engage in light activities such as yoga or walking in the evening to help your body wind down and prepare for sleep.

Lastly, if you find that sleep issues persist despite your best efforts, don't hesitate to seek professional guidance. Sleep disturbances can be a common challenge for those living with bipolar disorder, and a healthcare provider can offer tailored strategies or treatments to help you find balance. Remember, you are not alone in this journey, and taking steps to improve your sleep hygiene is a powerful way to support your mental health and overall stability. Embrace these strategies with patience and dedication, as each small step contributes to a more restful and rejuvenating night's sleep.

Chapter 5: Managing Medication

Understanding Your Treatment Plan

Understanding your treatment plan is a crucial step in managing bipolar disorder effectively. It can often feel overwhelming to navigate the complexities of medication, therapy, and lifestyle adjustments. However, by breaking down your treatment plan into manageable components, you can empower yourself to take control of your mental health journey. This understanding not only enhances your ability to cope but also fosters a sense of agency, allowing you to make informed decisions about your care.

Your treatment plan is uniquely tailored to you, reflecting your specific symptoms, triggers, and goals. It typically includes a combination of medication, therapy, and lifestyle changes. Medications, such as mood stabilizers or antipsychotics, can help regulate mood swings and reduce the intensity of episodes. Engaging in regular therapy sessions, whether cognitive behavioral therapy or other modalities, provides a safe space to explore your feelings and develop coping strategies. Remember, this collaborative approach is designed to support you in achieving stability and improving your overall quality of life.

As you familiarize yourself with each aspect of your treatment plan, it's essential to maintain open communication with your healthcare provider. Don't hesitate to ask questions about your medications and their potential side effects, or discuss any concerns that arise during therapy. Knowing what to expect can significantly reduce anxiety around treatment and help you feel more comfortable and confident in your choices. This proactive engagement is a key element in making your treatment plan work for you.

In addition to professional support, consider incorporating self-care practices into your daily routine. Regular exercise, a balanced diet, and sufficient sleep can significantly enhance your mood stability. Mindfulness techniques, such as meditation or journaling, can also serve as valuable tools for gaining insight into your emotions and managing stress. By prioritizing these self-care strategies, you reinforce the foundation of your treatment plan, giving yourself additional resources to cope with the challenges of bipolar disorder.

Ultimately, understanding your treatment plan is about building a partnership with yourself and your healthcare team. Embrace this opportunity to learn and grow, reminding yourself that you are not alone in this journey. With patience, persistence, and the right support, you can navigate the ups and downs of bipolar disorder, paving the way for a more stable and fulfilling life. Celebrate the small victories along the way, and trust in your ability to create a balanced existence amidst the challenges.

The Role of Medication

Medication can play a pivotal role in managing bipolar disorder, helping to stabilize mood swings and reduce the frequency and severity of episodes. For many individuals navigating this journey, finding the right medication can be a crucial step toward achieving a more balanced life. It's important to remember that while medication is a powerful tool, it is most effective when combined with other coping strategies, such as therapy, lifestyle changes, and strong support systems. Embracing medication as part of a holistic approach can empower you to take charge of your mental health.

Understanding how different medications work is essential. Mood stabilizers, antipsychotics, and antidepressants are commonly prescribed to help manage the ups and downs of bipolar disorder. Each person's experience with medication is unique, and it may take time to find the right combination that works for you. If you experience side effects or feel that your medication isn't effective, communicate openly with your healthcare provider. They can help adjust dosages or explore alternative options, ensuring that you are supported on this journey.

Consistency in taking medication is key. Developing a routine that incorporates your medication can help you stay on track and reduce the risk of missed doses. Some people find it helpful to use a pill organizer or set reminders on their phones. Establishing a connection between taking medication and other daily activities, such as brushing your teeth or having breakfast, can also reinforce this habit. Remember, every small step you take in maintaining your medication regimen is a step toward stability.

In addition to medication, integrating coping strategies into your daily life can enhance your overall well-being. Practices such as mindfulness, journaling, and regular physical activity can complement the effects of medication. These strategies not only provide additional support during challenging times but also empower you to manage stress and promote emotional resilience. Engaging in a supportive community, whether in-person or online, can also offer encouragement and understanding as you navigate your path.

Finally, it's important to celebrate your progress, no matter how small. Managing bipolar disorder is a journey filled with ups and downs, and acknowledging your efforts can reinforce your sense of agency. By embracing medication alongside effective coping strategies, you are taking significant steps toward building a stable and fulfilling life. Keep reminding yourself that you are not alone, and with patience and persistence, a balanced life is within reach.

Communicating with Your Doctor

Effective communication with your doctor is a cornerstone of managing bipolar disorder successfully. It can sometimes feel intimidating to discuss your symptoms, treatment options, or medication side effects, but remember that your doctor is there to support you. Building a trusting relationship with your healthcare provider can empower you to take an active role in your treatment journey. Start by being open and honest about your experiences, as this will allow your doctor to understand your unique situation better and tailor their approach to your needs.

Before your appointments, take some time to prepare. Write down any symptoms you've been experiencing, including changes in mood, energy levels, or sleep patterns. Note any questions or concerns you may have about your current treatment plan. This preparation not only helps you articulate your thoughts more clearly but also ensures that you don't forget to address crucial points during the consultation. Remember, your time with your doctor is valuable, and coming in well-prepared can lead to more productive discussions.

During your appointment, don't hesitate to share your feelings about how your treatment is affecting your daily life. If a medication isn't working well for you, or if you're experiencing unpleasant side effects, it's important to voice these concerns. Your doctor can't make necessary adjustments if they don't know what you're experiencing. Approach the conversation collaboratively; think of it as a partnership where both you and your doctor contribute to finding the best path forward for your health.

As you communicate, it's also essential to ask questions. If you don't understand a diagnosis or treatment recommendation, speak up. Phrasing your queries openly, such as "Can you explain why this medication is being recommended?" or "What are the potential side effects I should be aware of?" can lead to a more comprehensive understanding of your treatment plan. Your doctor is there to educate and guide you, and showing curiosity about your care can foster a more engaged and proactive approach.

Finally, remember that communication doesn't end with your appointments. Keep a record of your symptoms, mood changes, and any new concerns that arise between visits. This ongoing documentation can serve as a valuable tool for your next appointment, helping you to communicate more effectively. By taking these steps to enhance your communication with your doctor, you are actively participating in your health care and building a more stable foundation for managing bipolar disorder. Embrace this journey with confidence; every conversation is a step toward achieving balance and stability in your life.

Chapter 6: Developing Healthy Routines

Establishing Daily Structure

Establishing a daily structure is vital for anyone navigating the complexities of bipolar disorder. A consistent routine can provide a sense of stability and predictability, which are essential for managing mood swings and reducing anxiety. By developing a framework for your day, you can create an environment that fosters emotional balance. This structure does not have to be rigid; rather, it should serve as a flexible guide that allows for adjustments based on your mood and energy levels.

Start by identifying key activities that are important to you, such as work, exercise, social interactions, and self-care. These components should be woven into your daily routine to ensure a holistic approach to your well-being. Aim to allocate specific times for each activity, but remain open to modifying them as needed. For example, if you find that you're more productive in the morning, prioritize challenging tasks during that time. Remember, the goal is to create a rhythm that resonates with you and supports your mental health.

Incorporating small, achievable goals into your daily structure can significantly enhance your motivation and sense of accomplishment. Break larger tasks into manageable steps, allowing yourself to celebrate each completed task, no matter how small. This practice can help combat feelings of overwhelm and foster a positive mindset. Additionally, consider setting aside time for hobbies or activities that bring you joy, as they can serve as powerful mood boosters and a reminder of what you enjoy in life.

Consider using tools such as planners, apps, or calendars to help visualize your daily structure. These tools can serve as reminders and assist in maintaining your routine. You might find it helpful to color-code different activities or use symbols to denote various moods. This visual representation can make it easier to track your progress and adjust your routine as necessary. Remember, consistency is key, but flexibility is also essential to accommodate the ebbs and flows of your energy and emotions.

Lastly, communicate your daily structure with those around you, whether it be friends, family, or support groups. Sharing your plans can provide accountability and encourage others to support you in maintaining your routine. They can offer encouragement and even participate in activities with you, creating a sense of connection and community. Establishing a daily structure is not just about managing bipolar disorder; it's about fostering a life that feels grounded, purposeful, and fulfilling. Embrace this journey, and know that every step you take towards a structured day is a step towards greater stability in your life.

Nutrition and Mental Health

Nutrition plays a pivotal role in mental health, particularly for those navigating the challenges of bipolar disorder. The food we consume not only fuels our bodies but also significantly influences our mood and cognitive function. Research has shown that a balanced diet rich in whole foods, such as fruits, vegetables, whole grains, lean proteins, and healthy fats, can contribute to emotional stability. By being mindful of what we eat, we can empower ourselves to make choices that support our mental well-being and enhance our overall quality of life.

Incorporating omega-3 fatty acids, which are found in fish, flaxseeds, and walnuts, has been linked to improved mood regulation. These essential fats can help reduce inflammation and support brain health, making them a valuable addition to any diet. Similarly, foods rich in antioxidants, such as berries and leafy greens, can combat oxidative stress, which may play a role in mood disorders. By focusing on nutrient-dense foods, you can create a foundation that fosters resilience and stability.

It is essential to recognize that certain dietary patterns may exacerbate symptoms of bipolar disorder. Processed foods high in sugar and unhealthy fats can lead to fluctuations in energy and mood. By reducing the intake of these foods and replacing them with more nutritious options, you can create a more balanced internal environment. Establishing regular meal times and avoiding excessive caffeine and alcohol can also promote steadiness, allowing you to maintain a more even emotional state throughout the day.

Mindful eating can further enhance the connection between nutrition and mental health. Taking the time to savor meals, paying attention to how different foods affect your mood, and listening to your body's hunger cues can transform your relationship with food. This practice not only encourages healthier choices but also fosters a sense of control and awareness, which are vital when managing bipolar disorder. Engaging in meal preparation and planning can also serve as a therapeutic activity, providing a creative outlet and a sense of accomplishment.

Lastly, remember that nutrition is just one piece of the puzzle in managing bipolar disorder. It is most effective when combined with other coping strategies, such as therapy, medication, and support from loved ones. Embracing a holistic approach that includes nurturing your body through nutrition can significantly enhance your emotional resilience. By prioritizing your health and well-being, you are taking a proactive step toward building stability in your life, creating a nurturing environment that supports your mental health journey.

Setting Realistic Goals

Setting realistic goals is a crucial step toward managing the complexities of bipolar disorder. When living with this condition, it can be tempting to aim for lofty achievements that may feel out of reach. However, understanding the importance of setting attainable goals can provide a sense of direction and accomplishment, helping to build confidence and promote stability in your daily life. Remember, it's not about the size of the goal but the journey you take to achieve it.

Start by breaking your goals into smaller, manageable steps. This approach not only makes the process less overwhelming but also allows you to celebrate small victories along the way. For instance, instead of setting a goal to completely overhaul your daily routine, focus on one aspect at a time, such as establishing a consistent sleep schedule. These smaller, actionable steps can lead to significant improvements over time. Each achievement, no matter how minor it may seem, adds to your sense of capability and reinforces a positive mindset.

It's also essential to consider your current emotional and physical state when setting goals. Bipolar disorder can bring about fluctuations in mood and energy levels, which can impact your ability to pursue certain activities. Be kind to yourself by acknowledging these fluctuations and adapting your goals accordingly. If you're feeling particularly low, it may be more realistic to aim for short walks instead of lengthy workouts. Adjusting your goals to fit your current capacity allows you to remain motivated without setting yourself up for disappointment.

Accountability can be a powerful tool when striving to reach your goals. Sharing your objectives with trusted friends, family, or support groups can provide encouragement and keep you on track. These individuals can help remind you of your progress and offer support during challenging times. Additionally, consider journaling your goals and progress. This practice not only keeps you accountable but also gives you a tangible record of your journey, making it easier to reflect on your growth and resilience over time.

Finally, embrace the notion that setbacks are a natural part of any journey. If you find that you are unable to meet a goal, take a moment to reassess rather than dwell on frustration. Use these moments as learning experiences to adjust your approach for the future. Remember, the path to stability is not always linear, and every step you take, whether forward or backward, contributes to your overall growth. By setting realistic goals, you are equipping yourself with the tools to navigate life with bipolar disorder, fostering a sense of stability and hope for the future.

Chapter 7: Navigating Relationships

Maintaining Friendships

Maintaining friendships can be a rewarding yet challenging aspect of life for those managing bipolar disorder. Friendships provide essential support, camaraderie, and a sense of belonging, which can be particularly valuable during difficult times. However, the emotional fluctuations that come with bipolar disorder can strain relationships. Acknowledging these challenges is the first step toward nurturing and sustaining meaningful connections.

To maintain friendships, open communication is key. Sharing your experiences and the nature of your disorder with trusted friends can foster understanding and empathy. Let them know how they can support you during mood swings or difficult periods. This transparency can strengthen your bond and help your friends feel more equipped to be there for you. Remember, true friends will appreciate your honesty and willingness to share your journey.

Setting boundaries is another important aspect of maintaining friendships. It is crucial to communicate your needs and limitations, especially during episodes of mania or depression. Let your friends know when you may need space or when you are feeling overwhelmed. By establishing these boundaries, you create a safe environment for both yourself and your friends, allowing them to respect your needs while remaining engaged in the friendship.

Engaging in shared activities can also help sustain friendships. Whether it's a regular coffee date, a weekly walk, or a shared hobby, these moments of connection can create lasting memories and reinforce your bond. Finding activities that both you and your friends enjoy can provide a sense of normalcy and routine, which can be particularly beneficial during unpredictable times. Even small gestures, such as sending a text to check in or inviting a friend to join you in a fun activity, can go a long way in keeping the relationship vibrant.

Lastly, be gentle with yourself and your friends. Understand that maintaining friendships is a two-way street and requires effort from both parties. There may be times when you feel unable to engage or when a friend may not fully understand what you are going through. Acknowledging these hurdles and practicing patience can help you navigate the ups and downs of friendship. With commitment and care, you can cultivate lasting connections that enrich your life, reminding you that you are never alone in your journey.

Romantic Relationships and Bipolar Disorder

Romantic relationships can be both a source of joy and a challenge for individuals living with bipolar disorder. The intense emotions that often accompany this condition can enhance the highs of love but can also complicate the lows. Understanding how to navigate these emotional landscapes can empower you to build healthier, more fulfilling connections. Embracing the unique qualities you bring to a relationship allows you to create a partnership grounded in mutual understanding and respect.

Communication is a crucial element in any romantic relationship, but it takes on additional significance when bipolar disorder is part of the equation. Openly discussing your experiences, feelings, and the nature of your condition can foster a deeper connection with your partner. By sharing your journey, you help them understand your emotional fluctuations, making it easier for them to support you during challenging times. This transparency can reduce misunderstandings and build trust, creating a solid foundation for your relationship.

It's essential to develop coping strategies that work not only for you but also for your partner. Establishing routines can help create stability, which is particularly beneficial during mood swings. Consider setting aside regular time for each other, whether it's date nights or quiet evenings at home. Having these shared moments can strengthen your bond and provide both of you with something to look forward to, even during times when moods may shift unpredictably. Remember, consistency in your interactions can help mitigate the impact of mood changes.

Another important aspect of managing romantic relationships while living with bipolar disorder is self-care. Prioritizing your mental health not only benefits you but also contributes to the health of your relationship. Engage in activities that promote well-being, such as exercise, meditation, or pursuing hobbies. When you take care of yourself, you bring your best self into the relationship, enhancing your ability to support your partner and enjoy shared experiences. Celebrating small victories in your self-care journey can reinforce your resilience.

Ultimately, relationships require patience and effort from both partners. Bipolar disorder may introduce unique challenges, but it does not define your capacity for love and connection. By cultivating understanding, employing effective communication, and prioritizing self-care, you can nurture a romantic relationship that thrives despite the ups and downs. Embrace the journey, knowing that with dedication and love, you can build a steady ground that supports both you and your partner through life's challenges.

Family Dynamics

Family dynamics play a crucial role in the lives of those struggling with bipolar disorder. The relationships within a family can significantly influence emotional stability, support systems, and overall well-being. Understanding how these dynamics function can empower individuals to navigate their experiences more effectively. By fostering open communication and establishing healthy boundaries, families can create an environment that nurtures resilience and understanding.

It is important for families to recognize the unique challenges posed by bipolar disorder. Members may experience a wide range of emotions, from joy to frustration, often without warning. Acknowledging these fluctuations can help family members respond with empathy rather than judgment. By learning about the disorder together, families can build a collective knowledge base that encourages compassion and patience. This shared understanding can strengthen bonds and create a more supportive atmosphere.

Establishing routines can be a powerful tool in improving family dynamics. Predictability can provide a sense of stability for both the individual with bipolar disorder and their family members. Simple practices, such as regular family dinners or weekly check-ins, can foster connection and open lines of communication. These routines allow family members to share their experiences and feelings, reinforcing their commitment to one another. Moreover, predictable schedules can help manage mood swings and provide a sense of normalcy.

Conflict is inevitable in any family, but it can be particularly challenging for those grappling with bipolar disorder. Developing conflict-resolution strategies that prioritize understanding and respect can make a significant difference. Encouraging family members to express their feelings and concerns in a constructive manner can help de-escalate tensions. Implementing techniques like active listening and using "I" statements can transform potential arguments into productive discussions, ultimately strengthening family ties.

Lastly, it is essential for families to prioritize self-care. Supporting someone with bipolar disorder can be emotionally taxing, and caregivers often neglect their own well-being. Establishing individual self-care routines and encouraging each family member to pursue their interests can foster a healthier family environment. By taking care of themselves, family members can better support one another, creating a balanced dynamic that promotes stability. Together, families can navigate the complexities of bipolar disorder while building a foundation of love, understanding, and resilience.

Chapter 8: Coping with Crises

Recognizing When to Seek Help

Recognizing when to seek help is a pivotal skill for those navigating the complexities of bipolar disorder. Understanding your own limits and acknowledging when you're feeling overwhelmed can be a profound step toward maintaining stability. It's natural to experience ups and downs, but becoming aware of the signs that indicate you may need additional support can empower you. Trust your instincts; if you feel like your usual coping mechanisms aren't working, it's okay to reach out for help.

Pay attention to your emotional landscape. If you notice that your mood swings are more intense or frequent than usual, or if you find yourself feeling persistently low or unusually high, it may be time to consult with a mental health professional. Sometimes, these shifts can escalate into episodes that are difficult to manage alone. Recognizing the early signs of a potential crisis can make a significant difference in your ability to respond effectively and maintain stability. Remember, seeking help is a sign of strength, not weakness.

Physical symptoms can also be indicators that you should seek help. If you are experiencing changes in sleep patterns, appetite, or energy levels that seem out of the ordinary, these could signal a shift in your mental health. The mind and body are deeply connected, and taking notice of how you feel physically can provide valuable insights into your emotional well-being. Don't hesitate to discuss these changes with a healthcare provider; they can help you understand what's happening and develop a plan that works for you.

Another important aspect to consider is your daily functioning. If you find it increasingly difficult to complete everyday tasks, maintain relationships, or perform well at work or school, it's essential to evaluate your situation. These challenges may indicate that your current coping strategies aren't sufficient, and additional support could be beneficial. Remember that you do not have to face these challenges alone, and there are resources available to help you navigate this journey.

Finally, trust your support system. Friends and family can often notice changes in your behavior before you do. If someone close to you expresses concern, take their feedback seriously. Opening up about your struggles can foster understanding and create a support network that encourages you to seek professional help. Remember, you are not alone in this journey. Recognizing when to seek help is a vital skill that can lead to a more balanced and fulfilling life with bipolar disorder. Embracing this process is a crucial step toward building the steady ground you deserve.

Creating a Crisis Plan

Creating a crisis plan is an essential step for anyone navigating the complexities of bipolar disorder. This plan serves as a roadmap during challenging times, helping you maintain a sense of control and direction when emotions and situations feel overwhelming. Think of it as a safety net that you can rely on, a way to ensure you have the tools and support you need when the storms of life feel particularly fierce.

Begin by identifying your triggers—those specific situations, feelings, or events that can lead to a crisis. Recognizing these triggers is a powerful first step in managing your mental health. Once you have a clear understanding of what might set off a crisis, you can outline strategies to avoid or cope with these triggers. This might include creating a list of activities that help ground you or reaching out to a trusted friend or family member who can provide support when you need it most.

Next, consider what resources are available to you. This may include mental health professionals, helplines, or local support groups. Write down their contact information and keep it easily accessible. Having this information on hand can make a world of difference when you find yourself in a difficult situation. Additionally, think about how you can communicate your needs to those around you. Share your crisis plan with family and friends, and let them know how they can help you during tough times.

Incorporate self-care strategies into your crisis plan. These can be simple yet effective practices that bring you comfort and calm. Whether it's a favorite hobby, a short walk in nature, or mindfulness exercises, these activities can serve as a lifeline when you feel distress creeping in. Regularly engaging in self-care not only prepares you for potential crises but also builds resilience over time, making it easier to manage your emotions and reactions.

Finally, remember that a crisis plan is not static; it should evolve as you grow and change. Regularly review and update your plan, reflecting on what strategies have worked and what might need adjustment. This process of reflection and adaptation can empower you, reinforcing your ability to navigate the ups and downs of bipolar disorder. Know that you are not alone in this journey, and by taking proactive steps to create a crisis plan, you are investing in your well-being and fostering a sense of stability in your life.

Resources for Immediate Support

In moments of crisis, having access to immediate support can make all the difference for those living with bipolar disorder. Recognizing the signs of an impending mood episode is crucial, and knowing where to turn for help can empower you to take proactive steps. Whether you feel the weight of a depressive episode looming or the intensity of mania rising, resources are available to provide you with the assistance and reassurance you need. Remember, reaching out for help is a sign of strength, and it can pave the way for a more stable and fulfilling life.

One of the most effective resources for immediate support is a trusted mental health professional. If you already have a therapist or psychiatrist, don't hesitate to contact them during challenging times.

They are trained to help you navigate the ups and downs of bipolar disorder and can offer tailored strategies to manage your symptoms. If you don't have a provider, consider reaching out to helplines or mental health clinics in your area. Many organizations offer crisis intervention and can connect you with professionals who understand your needs.

Support groups can also play a significant role in providing immediate support. Whether in person or online, connecting with others who share similar experiences can foster a sense of community and understanding. These groups create a safe space where you can express your feelings without fear of judgment. Sharing your struggles and hearing how others cope can provide valuable insights and techniques that resonate with your personal journey. Remember, you are not alone in this, and there are people ready to support you.

In addition to professional help and support groups, utilizing digital resources can enhance your coping strategies. Many applications are designed specifically for individuals with bipolar disorder, offering mood tracking, mindfulness exercises, and coping strategies. These tools can help you gain insight into your mood patterns and provide immediate techniques to ground yourself during overwhelming moments. Explore various apps to find those that resonate with you, as they can serve as valuable companions on your journey toward stability.

Lastly, don't underestimate the power of your personal support network. Friends and family members who understand your condition can offer immediate comfort and encouragement. It can be helpful to communicate your needs to them, so they know how to best support you during difficult times. Whether it's a simple phone call, a walk in the park, or just sitting in silence together, the presence of loved ones can provide a sense of safety and stability. Remember, you deserve to lean on others and seek out the support that nourishes your well-being.

Chapter 9: Embracing Your Journey

Celebrating Small Victories

Celebrating small victories is an essential practice for anyone managing bipolar disorder. Each day presents a unique set of challenges, but it also offers opportunities to acknowledge progress, no matter how minor it may seem. Recognizing these small wins helps reinforce positive behavior and fosters a sense of accomplishment that can motivate you to keep moving forward. Whether it's getting out of bed, completing a task, or maintaining a stable mood for a few hours, each victory contributes to your overall well-being and recovery journey.

One effective way to celebrate small victories is to keep a journal dedicated to these moments. Every evening, take a few minutes to reflect on your day and jot down at least one thing you accomplished, no matter how small. This practice not only helps you focus on the positive aspects of your day but also creates a tangible record of your progress. Over time, you may be surprised at how many small victories accumulate, serving as a powerful reminder of your resilience and strength.

In addition to journaling, consider sharing your victories with supportive friends or family members. Opening up about your accomplishments can foster deeper connections and create a supportive environment where everyone celebrates each other's successes. When you share your victories, you invite others to acknowledge your efforts and provide positive reinforcement. This social support can be incredibly uplifting and can help you feel less isolated in your experience with bipolar disorder.

Another way to reinforce the significance of small victories is to create a rewards system for yourself. Set up a few simple rewards that you can treat yourself to when you achieve a small goal. Whether it's indulging in your favorite snack, watching a beloved movie, or taking a relaxing bath, these rewards can serve as a motivating factor. By associating small victories with enjoyable experiences, you reinforce the idea that your efforts are worthwhile and deserving of recognition.

Finally, remember that celebrating small victories does not diminish the larger challenges you face. Instead, it provides a framework to navigate your journey with greater positivity and hope. Acknowledging and celebrating even the smallest of wins helps shift your focus from what you struggle with to what you can achieve. Embrace this practice as an ongoing part of your life, and allow it to empower you as you continue to build stability in your bipolar life. Each celebration, no matter how small, is a step toward a more fulfilling and balanced existence.

Finding Meaning in the Struggle

Struggling with bipolar disorder can often feel like an overwhelming battle, but within that struggle lies the potential for profound personal growth and understanding. It is important to recognize that every challenge brings with it an opportunity for deeper insight into ourselves and our lives. When we face the ups and downs of this disorder, we are not merely enduring; we are engaging in a journey that can lead us to find meaning in our experiences. Embracing this perspective can transform the way we perceive our challenges and help us navigate the complexities of our emotions.

Finding meaning in the struggle begins with acceptance. Acknowledging that bipolar disorder is a part of your life does not mean you are defined by it. Instead, it allows you to explore how these experiences can contribute to your personal narrative. Acceptance opens the door to self-compassion, enabling you to treat yourself with kindness during the difficult times. It encourages you to view your struggles not as failures but as vital chapters in your story, each one teaching you something valuable about resilience, strength, and the human experience.

Another powerful aspect of finding meaning is the connection to others. Sharing your struggles with friends, family, or support groups can create a sense of belonging and understanding. It is through these connections that we often discover we are not alone in our experiences. Engaging with others who face similar battles can provide insights and perspectives that illuminate the path forward. These interactions can foster empathy, and compassion, and even inspire others to find meaning in their own challenges, creating a ripple effect that enhances the collective strength of the community.

Additionally, reflecting on your journey can uncover insights that may not be immediately apparent during times of turmoil. Journaling, meditation, or creative expression can serve as powerful tools for processing emotions and experiences. These practices allow you to explore the depths of your thoughts and feelings, helping you to identify patterns and triggers. By understanding your emotional landscape, you can begin to see how your struggles have shaped your character and contributed to your growth. This self-reflection can lead to clarity about your values and priorities, ultimately guiding you in setting goals that resonate with your authentic self.

Lastly, embracing the notion of growth through struggle empowers you to approach life with a sense of hope and purpose. Each challenge you face can be reframed as an opportunity to learn and evolve. By focusing on what you can control—your reactions, your mindset, and your choices—you can build a solid foundation of stability, even amidst the chaos. This proactive stance not only enhances your coping strategies but also instills a sense of agency in your journey. Remember, it is through the struggle that we often find the most profound meanings, and by embracing this truth, you are taking a significant step towards a life of greater fulfillment and stability.

Building Resilience

Building resilience is a vital aspect of managing bipolar disorder, as it empowers individuals to navigate the challenges they face with greater strength and confidence. Resilience does not mean the absence of struggle; rather, it involves developing the tools and mindset to bounce back from difficulties. When you embrace resilience, you cultivate a deeper understanding of your experiences and create a foundational strength that can support you during both manic and depressive episodes.

One of the key components of building resilience is fostering a strong support network. Surrounding yourself with understanding friends, family, and mental health professionals can provide the encouragement and resources needed to face life's ups and downs. Engaging in open conversations about your feelings and experiences helps to reduce isolation and reinforces the idea that you are not alone in your journey. Remember, it's okay to lean on others; sharing your burden can lighten the load and strengthen your resilience.

In addition to a supportive network, self-compassion is crucial for resilience. It is easy to be critical of oneself during challenging times, especially when managing bipolar disorder. However, practicing self-compassion involves treating yourself with the same kindness and understanding you would offer to a friend. Acknowledge your struggles without judgment and remind yourself that it's okay to have setbacks. This gentle approach fosters a positive mindset, allowing you to recover more swiftly from difficulties and reinforcing your resilience.

Developing coping strategies is another essential element in building resilience. Identify techniques that work for you, whether it's mindfulness practices, journaling, or engaging in creative outlets. Establishing routines can also provide a sense of predictability and control in your life. When you have a toolbox of coping strategies at your disposal, you empower yourself to manage your emotions and reactions more effectively, which can significantly enhance your resilience.

Finally, embrace the lessons that come from your experiences with bipolar disorder. Each challenge presents an opportunity for growth, and by reflecting on what you have learned, you can build a more resilient mindset. Celebrate your progress, no matter how small, and recognize your strength in facing adversity. By nurturing resilience, you not only improve your ability to cope with bipolar disorder but also build a richer, more fulfilling life. Remember, resilience is a journey, and every step you take brings you closer to steady ground.

Chapter 10: Looking Ahead

Setting Long-Term Goals

Setting long-term goals is a powerful practice that can bring clarity and purpose to your life, especially when navigating the challenges of bipolar disorder. It is essential to remember that having goals doesn't mean you need to have everything figured out right away. Instead, long-term goals offer a guiding light, helping you to stay focused on what truly matters to you, even during the ups and downs of your journey. By identifying what you want to achieve over the long haul, you create a sense of direction that can help you find stability.

To begin setting long-term goals, take some time to reflect on what is most important in your life. Consider your passions, values, and aspirations. These could range from personal growth and relationships to career ambitions and health objectives. Think about where you see yourself in five or ten years. Allow yourself the freedom to dream big, but also be realistic about your current circumstances. This balance is crucial; it helps ensure that your goals are both aspirational and achievable, providing you with a roadmap that is grounded in reality.

Once you've identified your long-term goals, break them down into smaller, manageable steps. This approach is particularly beneficial for individuals with bipolar disorder, as it can prevent feelings of overwhelm. Instead of fixating on the end result, focus on creating actionable steps that you can take on a daily or weekly basis. This method not only makes the goals feel more attainable but also allows you to celebrate small victories along the way, reinforcing a sense of accomplishment and motivation.

It's also important to remain flexible with your long-term goals. Life with bipolar disorder can be unpredictable, and there may be times when you need to adjust your goals based on your mental health status or external circumstances. Embracing change and being open to revising your goals can be liberating. Instead of viewing setbacks as failures, recognize them as opportunities to learn and adapt. By maintaining a flexible mindset, you can keep moving forward, even if the path looks different than you initially envisioned.

Finally, surround yourself with a support system that encourages your pursuit of these long-term goals. Share your aspirations with trusted friends, family members, or a therapist who can provide guidance, encouragement, and accountability. Engaging with others who understand your journey can be incredibly empowering. Remember, you are not alone in this process, and having people who cheer you on can make a significant difference in your ability to stay committed to your goals. Embrace the journey of setting and achieving long-term goals as a vital part of building stability in your life with bipolar disorder.

Continuing Education and Self-Help

Continuing education and self-help are vital components in managing bipolar disorder effectively. Engaging in ongoing learning allows individuals to gain a deeper understanding of their condition, empowering them to take control of their lives. Knowledge can demystify the symptoms and challenges of bipolar disorder, transforming how one navigates daily experiences. Consider seeking resources such as workshops, seminars, and support groups that focus on mental health. These platforms provide valuable information and foster a sense of community, reminding you that you are not alone in your journey.

Self-help strategies complement formal education by offering practical tools for everyday coping. Journaling, for instance, is a powerful way to track moods, identify triggers, and reflect on experiences. This practice can lead to greater self-awareness and serve as an invaluable resource when discussing your condition with healthcare professionals. Additionally, mindfulness techniques, such as meditation and deep-breathing exercises, can help ground you during moments of distress, allowing for a clearer perspective and a calmer mind.

Engaging with literature focused on bipolar disorder can also be transformative. Many authors share their personal stories, offering insights and strategies that have worked for them. These narratives can inspire hope and resilience, reminding you that recovery is a journey filled with ups and downs. Seek out books, articles, and online resources that resonate with you, as they can provide guidance and encouragement when facing challenges. The more you read and learn, the more equipped you become to manage your symptoms and navigate life's complexities.

Consider incorporating courses that focus on emotional regulation and cognitive-behavioral therapy techniques into your routine. Many organizations offer online classes tailored to those living with bipolar disorder, where you can learn coping mechanisms and strategies in a supportive environment. These educational opportunities can enhance your skill set, making it easier to handle stress and emotional upheaval. Remember, investing in your education is an investment in your well-being, and every step you take brings you closer to stability.

Finally, surrounding yourself with a supportive community can greatly enhance your self-help efforts. Whether through local support groups or online forums, connecting with others who share similar experiences can provide comfort and motivation. Sharing your struggles and successes fosters a sense of belonging and reinforces the idea that recovery is possible. Together, you can exchange tips, celebrate milestones, and offer encouragement, creating a network of strength that can help you remain steady on your path to mental wellness. Embrace the journey of continuing education and self-help as a powerful means of building stability in your life.

Inspiring Stories of Recovery

In the journey of managing bipolar disorder, stories of recovery can serve as powerful reminders of hope and resilience. One such story is that of Sarah, a young woman who faced the daunting challenges of the disorder head-on. After years of navigating the ups and downs, she discovered the transformative power of community support. By joining a local support group, Sarah found a network of individuals who understood her struggles and celebrated her victories. Through shared experiences, she learned valuable coping strategies, such as mindfulness and journaling, which became integral to her daily routine. Sarah's journey exemplifies how connection can illuminate the path toward stability and healing.

Another inspiring story is that of David, a musician who channeled his experiences with bipolar disorder into his art. Initially, his mood swings led him to question his talent and purpose, but he eventually realized that his emotions could fuel his creativity. David began to write songs that reflected his experiences, using music as a therapeutic outlet. This not only provided him with a sense of accomplishment but also helped him process his feelings. By sharing his music with others, he found a sense of belonging and purpose, inspiring listeners who faced similar struggles. David's story shows that embracing one's passion can be a powerful coping mechanism, turning pain into purpose.

Then there is the story of Maria, a mother of three who battled bipolar disorder while navigating the complexities of parenthood. Maria faced significant challenges, especially during manic and depressive episodes, but she was determined not to let her condition define her. She sought therapy and medication, which helped stabilize her mood. Additionally, Maria developed a structured daily routine that included self-care practices like yoga and meditation. By prioritizing her mental health, she was able to be more present for her children and create a nurturing home environment. Maria's dedication to her family and her own well-being highlights the importance of self-care and the impact it can have on loved ones.

Mark, a corporate professional, shares his journey of recovery through workplace accommodations. After disclosing his bipolar diagnosis to his employer, he was able to access resources tailored to his needs, such as flexible hours and mental health days. This support allowed him to maintain a successful career while managing his condition. Mark also emphasizes the importance of breaking the stigma surrounding mental health in the workplace, advocating for open conversations about mental health challenges. His story serves as a reminder that seeking help and support in professional settings can lead to positive outcomes and a more balanced life.

Lastly, there is the story of Emily, who turned her struggles into advocacy. After years of feeling isolated, she became involved in mental health awareness campaigns and started a blog chronicling her experiences with bipolar disorder. Through her writing, Emily found her voice and empowered others to share their stories. She emphasizes that recovery is not a linear process, but rather a series of ups and downs that can be managed with perseverance and support. Emily's journey illustrates the importance of using one's voice to inspire and uplift others, creating a ripple effect of hope in the bipolar community. Each of these stories reminds us that recovery is possible, and with the right tools and support, a fulfilling life is within reach.

9 798343 253580